# Hailsham

# in old picture postcards

by
Hailsham Historical and Natural History Society

European Library – Zaltbommel/Netherlands

**BACK IN TIME**

ISBN10: 90 288 3056 1
ISBN13: 978 90 288 3056 1

© 1984 European Library – Zaltbommel/Netherlands
© 2010 Reprint of the fourth edition of 1991

European Library
post office box 49
NL – 5300 AA Zaltbommel/The Netherlands
telephone: 0031 418 513144
fax: 0031 418 515515
e-mail:publisher@eurobib.nl

# INTRODUCTION

The parish of Hailsham lies on the edge of Pevensey Marsh some 7 miles north of Eastbourne and 12 miles east of Lewes. At one time it contained the parish of Polegate, an erstwhile hamlet to the south which had grown round the railway junction which expanded so rapidly in the inter-war years that it was separated from its mother parish in 1937.

Except for the alluvial marsh and a portion in the north-east on Tunbridge Wells sand Hailsham is on Weald clay. Until the 1939-1945 War the surrounding agriculture was mainly dairy farming but much land has gone under the plough since 1950 and several small dairy farms on the town's outskirts have disappeared under bricks and mortar.

Why a village should grow at a particular place is always an interesting question and in the case of Hailsham it is not easy to pinpoint why our early ancestors settled here. Although the Romans were in Pevensey Castle no Roman remains have been found in the parish.

Pevensey Marsh in Roman and Saxon times, if not actually under water, was at least a vast swamp. Nearly all the old lanes and tracks running north-west from Pevensey converge on Hailsham. The site of the church on its hill suggests an ancient place of pagan worship.

The name Hailsham is Saxon, derived from Haegels ham — the homestead or clearing made by a Saxon called Haegel. By the time of the Domesday Book in 1087 the name had been corrupted to Hamelsham.

Domesday Book tells that a certain William held 1½ hides (about 180 acres) from the Count of Mortain, that there was land for 4 ploughs and there were 4 smallholders with 1 ox. There were 13 salthouses or saltpans of which the Count had kept 11 for himself. Hailsham was assessed at 110 shillings before 1066 but at only 20 shillings in 1087 so Hailsham had suffered as a result of the Norman invasion.

In the adjacent manor of Bowley in the eastern part of the parish William also held ½ hide from the Count. There was land for 2 ploughs, 2 villagers and 1 smallholder, 8 acres of meadow and 4 salthouses. Its value rose from 15 shillings in 1066 to 30 shillings in 1087.

By 1229 Hailsham had a church. Whether this was of wood or stone we do not know but it was rebuilt, together with its tower, by the mid-fifteenth century. In 1252 a market charter was granted so the village was beginning to assume some importance.

There are 70 houses listed in the Hearth Tax Assessments of 1662 suggesting a population of about 320 at that date. It was during the nineteenth century that the town started to grow, the population swelling from 897 in 1801 to 3,369 in 1891. Although the town itself was growing, it is generally recognised that the surrounding countryside was stagnating. The reasons for this are various, the chief ones being the employment given by the newly introduced rope and string industry and the appearance of the railway in 1849. The market in cattle and corn restarted in 1786 after being dormant for some 150 years and it quickly became one of the largest in Sussex. The enclosure of the Common in 1855 opened up new land for building on the south side of the town.

The town has been fortunate in its chroniclers. In 1884 Thomas Geering, a currier by trade, published his series of essays entitled 'Our Parish. A medley by one who has never lived out of it'. At the same period Edwin Isaac Baker lived at 21, High Street. He was a professional photographer of great skill and took many photographs of the town and surrounding area. In 1901 a young man called Louis F. Salzmann, who was staying with his aunt at Downford at the time, wrote his 'History of Hailsham' which is a mine of information to antiquarians and those interested in manorial history. Salzmann later made an international reputation as a historian.

Harking back to the days when Hailsham was dominated by the barracks, Geering wrote *The history of our parish in the present century may be summarised in two words, viz. the barrack yard and the brick yard. Then we were military and stagnant, now we are social and progressive. Then we were roused by the drum and trumpet; now by the ring of the trowel and the rattle of the saw.* We venture to suggest that these words are as true now as the day upon which they were written.

The neighbouring parish of Hellingly includes Upper and Lower Horsebridge and Upper and Lower Dicker. Along much of the boundary with Hailsham it is so built up that it is difficult to separate the two parishes.

The chief glory of Hellingly can be said to be its church, churchyard and picturesque group of surrounding cottages. The circular churchyard indicates that it was almost certainly a pre-christian place of worship. The original church apparently was cruciform and is of great age, containing much Norman work. Horsefield records that it had 'a mean wooden spire and a good peal of six bells' but a battlemented tower was built in 1836 and the clock added in 1837 to commemorate the accession of Queen Victoria.

The stiff yellow clay upon which a good deal of the parish stands gave rise to the local industries of pottery, brick and tile making but sadly these have now died out.

When the Dicker Common was enclosed early in the nineteenth century thousands of oaks, including 600 mature trees, were destroyed. The geometric grid of fields along the A22 road at this point shows very clearly the effects of the enclosure award. The old road to London skirted the edge of the common but with enclosure also came the turnpike and the modern A22 road was formed.

On this stretch of road may be seen the unique Bow Bells milestones embellished with representations of the Bow Bells and the number of miles to travel to reach them. Where the road runs through the former Pelham estates the Pelham buckle is added.

1. The first recorded mention of a church at Hailsham is in 1229 but the present building is fifteenth century, substantially rebuilt and restored in Victorian times. Almost all the windows were destroyed by bomb blast in 1943. Five of the peal of eight bells date from 1663 — one being recast in 1768 — and three from 1889. The earlier bells were cast by John Hodson — probably at the place now called Bellbanks. The bells were taken down in 1951, the four lighter ones being recast and the four heavier ones retuned. The custom of ringing the curfew at eight o'clock each evening was maintained until the outbreak of the 1939-1945 War. The present clock was installed to celebrate Queen Victoria's Diamond Jubilee. Until then, the tower had a single diamond shaped clock face with only one hand, the intervals between the numerals being divided into four quarters instead of five minutes.

2. Looking south along the High Street at the turn of the century, the large house on the right was known as The Acacias and at an earlier period was the home of Thomas Burfield who founded his Rope Works in 1807. Next door was Headcorn House, the shop of Tassell, grocer and draper. The display of goods on the highway opposite, which would not be tolerated under modern traffic conditions, belonged to A.F. Smith, ironmonger, and next to it was the Brewers Arms. Both these buildings were badly damaged by fire in 1928. The properties backing on to the churchyard at one time belonged to Charles I and were sold by Cromwell's Parliament in 1646. There exists a list of the properties, their tenants and the rents paid. One property is recorded as being tenanted as early as the reign of Richard III. There is evidence to show that these buildings were erected over the old burial ground.

3. The Crown Hotel is reputed to be the oldest, and at one time the principal, inn of Hailsham and this photograph shows its front wall carrying a number of posters for Cavendish and Dodson, the Liberal candidates at the 1868 parliamentary election. Of interest is the man wearing a Sussex round frock. This garment is sometimes incorrectly described as a smock but there is a vital difference in that the round frock was the same back and front with a small neck opening of about three inches whereas the coat-type smock opened further down the front. The Sussex agricultural or manual worker would wear a round frock made of heavy quality material for work and a garment of much finer quality material with smocking for Sundays and special occasions.

4. Progress in transport is well illustrated in this view of the Crown Hotel showing the old 'penny-farthing' next to the new 'safety bicycle'. A typical price for a 'penny-farthing' between 1871 and 1880 was £8, with an extra £4 if it had gears, while a typical price for a 'safety bicycle' between 1881 and 1890 was £7.50; this was at a time when a labourer's weekly wage was less than £1. The story goes that a challenge was made between the proud owner of a new 'safety bicycle' and the owner of a 'penny-farthing' for a race to Union Corner (at the bottom of Hawks Road) and back, the 'safety bicycle' of course winning easily. The fine wrought iron sign, which was in existence until the 1939-1945 War, was made in the early 1800's by a blacksmith called Ellis who had a shop in the High Street.

WAR MEMORIAL, HAILSHAM

5. At a public meeting it was resolved to erect a monument in honour of those Hailsham residents who lost their lives in the service of their country during the 1914-1918 War, to erect a Memorial Hall and to provide an Institute in which the returned servicemen and inhabitants of Hailsham could meet on common ground under happier social conditions. Mr. J.S.O. Robertson-Luxford donated part of the Vicarage Field as a site for the Monument and Hall while South View in Western Road was given by two donors for a Public Library and Institute. The Memorial Hall was demolished and replaced by the Hailsham Club building when the Vicarage Field shopping precinct was built in the 1960's. The War Memorial was unveiled on 28th November, 1920 by Lord Leconfield, the then Lord Lieutenant of the County.

6. In a deed of 1803, 'William Stevens of Berwick and G. Woger of Alfriston who are about to build a house in the field, now Mr. Benjamin Shelley's near the barracks on Hailsham Common - - - bind themselves to Mr. Isaac Clapson, gent, that Richard Wood, innkeeper, of Hailsham shall have a half share of the business.' This was the beginning of The Grenadier Hotel, built to supply beer to the soldiers stationed at the barracks which then stood on the western side of Eastwell Place. Thomas Geering records that after the barracks ceased to be used the Grenadier rapidly became the rendezvous for every tramp within ten miles. He said 'a merrier lot never existed.' This picture shows the Grenadier being refaced in 1910.

7. The buildings in this picture are virtually unchanged externally to this day. The one on the left was erected in the mid-nineteenth century and was used for the manufacture of mineral water. They stand on North Street which originally was known as Back Lane, but a well-to-do resident objected to this name on his mail and it became Terminus Road. In 1894 the newly formed Parish Council officially named the road North Street. Standing on the step at Kirby Croft is Mr. David Guy, Auctioneer, Supt. Registrar, Assistant Overseer to the Union, Secretary to the Gas Board Company and the Hailsham Building Society and a man of many parts. The brake in the foreground would hold fifteen passengers and a considerable amount of baggage and was in great demand between Hailsham and Heathfield, particularly on market day.

8. Cortlandt, built in 1793 and previously known as New House, was the home of John Bristow who died in 1803. In that year a Barracks was built in Hailsham to accommodate troops stationed in the town ready for the threatened Napoleonic invasion. The Barrack Master was Philip van Cortlandt, a former American Royalist Officer, who was accommodated at New House and who died in 1814 at about the same time as the Barracks ceased to exist. The house was bought in 1881 by William Strickland who added two new wings and re-named it Cortlandt. When he died in 1918 he left the property to his widow on condition that she did not re-marry and that she continued to live there. Upon her death in 1932 the house was purchased by Hailsham R.D.C. for offices and they and Wealden District Council continued to use it for this purpose until 1982.

9. In 1881 William Strickland purchased an area of land opposite Cortlandt and laid out Victoria Road on part of it, keeping the section fronting George Street for the establishment of a deer paddock on which he kept three head of deer — a stag and two does — together with a pair of peacocks. A brick and tile shelter for the animals was erected with a central clock tower and the clock was illuminated by gas in 1887 to commemorate Queen Victoria's Diamond Jubilee. The building was demolished in the 1930's and the clock was eventually re-built and installed in the window of the Hailsham Historical and Natural History Society Museum in Western Road. An office building was erected on the site for the Sussex River Authority and subsequently the Police Station moved there from its previous home adjacent to the Magistrates' Court.

10. The exact age of The George Hotel is not known because, although its frontage is eighteenth century, there is evidence of older work inside. It has always been one of the leading inns of the town and was famous for its 'market ordinaries', i.e. dinners for farmers attending the market when such a visit involved a whole day out. It was also the hostelry where one went to hire a fly, post chaise or other means of conveyance. A billiards room was another of the amenities it provided. Until the present Magistrates Courts were built in 1861 the Petty Sessions were held in two upstairs rooms at The George. The landlord in the 1830's was James Bray Baker, a cricketer of county standard who is credited with winning a single wicket match against eleven Eastbourne players with one William Martin, a shoemaker, to field for him.

11. This photograph shows the old fifteenth century house at the corner of High Street and George Street. At one time there was a gallery where the first floor jetty overhangs the George Street footpath but this had to be removed because it was a hazard to coaches turning the corner. Nearby in Market Square stood a Market Cross — similar, it is said, to that still standing in Alfriston. This, too, was removed as a traffic hazard in the early nineteenth century and unfortunately there are no paintings or engravings of it. The stores in front of which three ladies are standing was the original site of the Crown Hotel, which stood there until about 1780. When the building was re-built in the 1970's a Tudor stone archway and fireplace were exposed.

12. The building at the corner of High Street and George Street is now seen as it was in the early 1920's. It was demolished in 1935 and a new building was erected on the site for the Westminster Bank, which became the National Westminster Bank in the late 1960's upon amalgamation with the National Provincial Bank. The building beyond the horse and cart on the left hand side of the photograph at one time was the site of a blacksmith's shop. In the background can be seen some of the trees in the Deer Paddock. Among the group of children posing for the photographer can be seen a boy with his iron hoop, a popular possession of boys at that time. One Hailsham resident recalls rolling his hoop all the way to Eastbourne and back — he says it helped to make the journey seem shorter.

13. St. Mary's, the facing building on the right of the picture, had a seventeenth century frontage and this view shows several windows which had been bricked up following the introduction of the Window Tax in 1696. The rear part was much older and, during alterations, the date 1583 was found cut into a beam. The house on the left, adjoining the churchyard, was a butcher's shop for over a hundred years and the right-hand side of the house became one of Hailsham's first banks — the London and County. The present Estate Agents building replaced it in 1909. In the first part of the nineteenth century, when the butcher's shop was kept by a man named Kennett, one of his customers was the local doctor, Dr. Long. His daily order never varied throughout the year — always one and a half pounds of beef steak which he had made into a pudding.

14. About 1540 a building was erected in Market Street which was an inn known as the Fleur-de-Lys until 1762 when it was acquired by the parish and became the Poor House until 1854. Later the northern end of the building was used as the Post Office and the southern end as an undertakers and wheelwright's shop. The picture shows the wheelwright's shop in 1889 after it had been badly damaged by fire despite the efforts of the Hailsham and Eastbourne Fire Brigades. The Post Office part of the building was repaired and became a private dwelling while the remainder was demolished and a new building erected which became the Fire Station until the present Fire Station was built in Victoria Road in the 1960's. The flat-roofed building to the right of the picture was Christians Tea-room; it was badly damaged by a bomb during an air raid in 1943 and had to be demolished.

15. In Marshfoot Lane, about one mile from the Vicarage and at the end of the ridge where it begins to slope down towards sea level, stood Marshfoot House which dated back at least to the sixteenth century and possibly much earlier. The building was demolished around the end of the nineteenth century. Tradition says it was a grange of Wilmington Priory but it is more likely to have been connected with either Bayham or Michelham. By 1860 it had been divided into four somewhat primitive homes for labourers' families and, although much rebuilt when this photograph was taken, it still retained evidence of its age in its thick sandstone walls, small stone-cased windows and steep roof. The pond by the side of the lane is said to have been used by the smugglers coming up from Pevensey Bay as a hiding place for their kegs of spirit.

16. Common Pond stands on what was common land owned by the Lord of the Manor. One of the earliest records is an entry in the Sussex Assize Roll 1263 which states *Gilbert, son of Gilbert Godseb, while bathing in the pond at Haylesham, was drowned and Salomon, son of John Russel, who first found him is not suspected.* When the Common was enclosed in 1855 the Lord of the Manor, Lord Sackville, retained ownership, the pond and an area of land around it being leased out. In 1921 Hailsham Parish Council asked Lord Sackville if he was prepared to sell the pond to the Council and in 1922 he offered it to them for £300, the Council purchasing it with the help of private subscribers. The part of the Common near the pond was known as The Butts. In bygone times, when it was compulsory for the men of England to learn and practice the art of using the longbow, it was on this part of the Common that the men of Hailsham practiced.

17. This view of the shop of A.F. Smith, the ironmonger, was taken about 1880 when he occupied the only three-storeyed premises in the High Street backing on to the churchyard. As can be seen from the advertising over the shop, the range of goods stocked extended far beyond that of the modern ironmonger, including such diverse items as beds and bedding and dairy utensils. At that time there were few specialist shops selling the various new inventions coming on to the market and ironmongers tended to be astute business men who would take these new developments in their stride. The photograph shows bassinettes for sale outside the shop while in the window can be seen a number of tennis racquets.

18. This picture of George Street taken sometime between 1890 and 1900 shows the shop of Barnett the ironmonger which today is occupied by the Sussex County Building Society. Until about 1870 it housed the Post Office; at that time there was no shop window or shop space for the public to enter, transactions being conducted by the Postmaster over a half-door while his customers stood on the footway outside. The building at the left of the picture with two small round windows occupied the site of The Pavilion, which was to become Hailsham's first and only purpose-built cinema. The house next to Barnett's shop was known as Roseneath and was the home of Dr. Gould.

19. This picture shows the 1898 Christmas display at Lovell's butchers 15, High Street. At this time of year the butchers vied with each other in their elaborate displays of Christmas fare. Once the arrangement was completed it was left in position until sold and a night watchman was employed to guard it. One imagines the reaction of present day public health inspectors. One ambition was to show the carcasses of prize winning fatstock from the local show. The drainpipe on the left is decorated with rabbits but what was the purpose of the cage of live fowls — eggs while you wait? The week before Christmas the butcher would invite good customers along one evening; the Hailsham Band would play seasonal music and free drinks would be handed round by the butcher.

George Street, Hailsham. *With love and all abo...*

20. Thomas White opened a grocer's shop in Market Square in 1816. By 1870 the business had prospered and we find Daniel White described as 'wholesale and retail grocer, tailor, draper, hatter, wine and spirit merchant, purveyor of china, glass and earthenware and Agent for Norwich Union Fire and Life'. Such shops were a necessary part of the distributive trade when goods travelled by horse and rail transport. They provided a chain of depots from which other villages further from the railway could draw their supplies. Apart from being a shop keeper he was also responsible for issuing Government licences for hawkers, guns, male servants, carriages, horses and mules, armorial bearings, horse dealers, dogs, gamekeepers and game. At one time the building was the home of Anthony Trumble, Under Sheriff of Sussex, who died in 1733 and is buried in Hailsham churchyard.

21. Here is the studio of Edwin Isaac Baker who for thirty years was bookseller, photographer, stationers, newsagent and lending librarian at 21, High Street, now Pipers the newsagent. Mr. Baker was a great friend of Thomas Geering, whose articles he read before publication and he also took the photographs for 'Our Parish', published 1885. His son, Ernest Baker, went to be a Baptist clergyman in South Africa and Mr. Baker compiled a volume of photographs to send to him. Mr. Baker was enough of a business man to recognise their commercial possibilities and many of the pictures in this volume were on sale as framed photographs and picture postcards. Today these pictures provide a living history of this part of Sussex, the villages, houses, churches and people.

22. The shop in the centre of this High Street view of about 1880 belongs to Jenner, druggist, who can be seen standing by his doorway. It is known to have been a chemist's shop since 1804 and provides the same service to-day. A bootscraper can be clearly seen by the front door of the adjoining house and the shop beyond was occupied by Colbran, clocksmith; it is reputed to have been the first purpose-built shop front in Hailsham. The next shop was that of E.I. Baker, who is the middle one of the three men standing by his door. In the old house behind the shop near the right hand side of the picture Captain Barclay was billeted in 1804. He was renowned throughout England for his strength and athletic prowess, his crowning exploit being a walk of 1,000 miles in 1,000 hours for which he is said to have netted £16,000 in wagers.

23. In the nineteenth century most towns had their own brewery and Hailsham was no exception. Thomas Gooche started a brewery in 1827 in Brewery Road, now Battle Road. His strong ales were well known and in great demand in the district. By 1871 Robert Overy employed five men at the brewery and owned three beerhouses out of the fourteen inns and beerhouses in the area. Unlike today the cost of living remained fairly static in the last century and the price of beer stayed at 5p. per gallon for over fifty years. The fine new brick building, shown in the picture, was erected by Mr. Olney in 1887 and today is occupied by Apaseal. The building on the right was the home of the brewer and part of the loft over the stables was used as a Catholic place of worship from 1917 to 1922.

24. In 1861 a building was erected at the junction of High Street and Battle Road comprising a Court Room together with an office and residence for the Police Superintendent. Petty Sessions were held in the Court Room on alternate Wednesdays. The photograph shows the entire strength of the local police force, which covered a wide area including Pevensey and Westham, comprising the Superintendent, one sergeant and twelve constables. Also in the picture are the Superintendent's family and gig. The exact date of the photograph is not known but it could not be before 1868 because the Methodist Church, which can just be seen at the right of the picture, was built in that year.

25. The Hailsham Volunteer Fire Brigade was formed in 1877 as a result of a Parish Meeting, the first machine (seen here) being loaned by Mr. William Strickland, a local corn merchant who resided at Cortlandt and who was the Hon. Captain of the Fire Brigade. He is seen on the extreme right of the picture. In the event of a fire the volunteers were summoned by a firebell which used to hang under a gable at Cortlandt. The machine was housed at the Terminus Hotel and horsed by horses stabled there. Later it was horsed by a local undertaker and it is said to be not unknown for a funeral to be interrupted on the alarm being raised when the horses were removed from the funeral carriage.

26. Hailsham became a 'post town' in 1673, i.e. mail was sent there from London for subsequent distribution in the surrounding area. Until quite late in the nineteenth century mail for places such as Pevensey was not delivered but had to be collected from Hailsham. About 1812, Hailsham was told that, unless the road from Horsebridge was repaired, the mail would only come as far as there. This photograph was taken in 1908 outside the building at the junction of Vicarage Road and Market Square nowadays occupied by the Midland Bank. It was Hailsham's first purpose-built Post Office and was erected privately by the Postmaster in 1899.

27. Seen here is Mr. T. Boniface, who is believed to have been Hailham's first dustman. The lettering on the headboard of his cart refers to him as Town Dustman. This was a private service not chargeable to the rates and was most desirable because there are frequent references in the Vestry Minutes of the mid-nineteenth century to the nuisance caused by householders stacking their ashes and middens in the road. A similar service was provided for the watering of roads in the summer to lay the dust — there being no tarmac surfacing in those days; the charge for this service was one penny per week per house. This photograph was taken in North Street and on the right can be seen the houses which were demolished in the late 1960's to provide a site for a public car park.

28. Before the advent of the petrol engine all goods for outlying districts were distributed by horse-drawn carts and wagons. We see here that Messrs. Isted and Harris of Herstmonceux were carriers delivering daily in Herstmonceux, Laughton, Ringmer and Lewes but only on Saturdays in Hailsham. They were one of several such firms in the neighbourhood. Before the coming of the railways the two Hailsham carriers Hilder and Hoad sent their wagons to London twice a week and in 1844 the business card of Hoad (who lived where the National Westminster Bank stands today) stated ...*wagons, vans and carts are kept to convey furniture and luggage to any part of England... carts kept to fetch and carry goods to any part of the Metropolis.*

29. The smock mill in Mill Road was known variously as Lower Mill, Hamlins, Mercer's or Catt's. David Catt was apprenticed to John Mercer and was one of three partners in the mill from 1879 to 1886, after which he took complete control of the mill and the associated bakery business. A hundred years ago there were probably as many as a dozen mills within three or four miles of Hailsham. As each farmer threshed his corn, so he would take a wagon load to his local mill for grinding for feeding his stock. Local ground oats was a staple food for poultry fattening for which this area was well known. The mill was destroyed by fire in November, 1923 and was rebuilt with an engine replacing the wind-driven sweeps. Fire struck again in 1969 but this time the mill was not rebuilt.

HAREBEATING MILL, SUSSEX.

30. This post mill, known as Kenwards or Upper Mill, was in a field at the rear of the Methodist Church. In August 1869 it was bought by Robert Thomas Martin and four months later the miller, John Grove Kenward, became enmeshed in the machinery and was killed. Mr. Martin was extremely distressed by the accident and he more or less gave away the windmill on the understanding it was taken down and removed. So it passed into the ownership of George Weller who dismantled and re-erected it on top of a two-storey roundhouse at Harebeating Lane, renaming it Harebeating Mill. The four shuttered sweeps had a span of over seventy feet. The sweeps were removed in 1918 and in 1934 the smock tower collapsed. The brick roundhouse, however, still survives.

31. In the latter part of the nineteenth century about 25% of the population of Hailsham was engaged in agriculture. Haymaking was carried out completely by hand and this is well illustrated in this photograph of grass cutting at Cacklebury — the South Road area of Hailsham. Normally there were four men to a team, each with a scythe and wearing a leather belt with a cloth and a stone rubber at the back for blade sharpening. Trousers were strapped up above the calf, the straps being known as Nollegers, Knot-leggers or Yorks. Each man would have with him a basket of 'bait' together with a stone jar of beer which was often provided by the farmer. The men would scythe for days on end making it look quite effortless but in fact it was back-breaking work.

32. Grass cutting was the first stage in the haymaking process and, as soon as the cut grass was ready, women and children would come and help to turn over and shake the grass. After a few days of sun the hay would be ready to be picked up. Pitchforks were used to throw it on to the hay-cart where it was expertly handled by the loader. The drudgery of the task was partially offset by a liberal allowance of 'haying' beer supplied by the employer. The view of the church tower in the top right-hand corners identifies this typical scene as being in Parsonage Field, better known as Vicarage Field, which nowadays is the site of a shopping precinct and public car park.

33. Eventually grass cutting became less arduous when mowing machines drawn by horses were introduced to replace the hand mowing. The type of machine shown remained in use right up to the time when the modern mechanical mower came into use. If the crop was good and heavy, it was very hard work for a single pair of horses to keep going all day so it was quite a common practice to use one pair of horses for the morning and another pair for the afternoon. As tractors gradually began to replace the horse for agricultural work the farmers sometimes converted their horse-drawn implements by replacing the horse shafts with home-made tow bars.

34. The Sussex wagon, which has been described the best of all Shire wagons, was strongly built with broad wheels to enable it to be pulled through the heavy clay. Its length and strength enabled it to carry large and heavy loads yet the shape of its body permitted better than average manoeuvrability. Colour and style of paintwork helped to identify the county of origin, Sussex wagons having blue bodies and red wheels. The smaller vehicle is a tip, or 'dung', cart which had a pin at the front which could be removed to enable the body to be tipped backwards to empty the contents. The carts and machines made for use with the plodding horse did not stand up well to the speed and snatching of tractors when these were introduced on the farms and it was not long before they fell into disrepair and disuse being seen nowadays mainly in museums.

35. Thomas Burfield, a saddler and collar maker, was in business in Hailsham High Street. He bought his rope and cord from London but in 1807 decided to manufacture his own – thus starting the rope industry in Hailsham. On the right of the picture is one of his spinning walks, which was behind his High Street shop (demolished 1956 and now the site of Woolworth's). By 1887 the business had expanded enormously and amongst other things was producing hop bags, coal sacks, wagon and gig covers, halters, clothes lines, mats and door mats and employing two hundred hands. Cassells magazine, 1st June 1898 states *The ropemaker is a noted person. All the ropes for capital punishment used by the government at home and in the colonies are made in Hailsham. Every rope during the present century used at Newgate, was made here.*

36. When Thomas Burfield first started rope making the work was done by outworkers. They would take the completed rope in wheelbarrows on a Friday to a warehouse in the High Street when they would be paid and collect the raw materials for the next week's work. The work was done on eight ropewalks around the town, all of which were on land belonging to Burfield and were in use until the early 1900's. The outworkers were paid piece-work rates and, since all the work was outdoors and could not be carried out in wet weather, their income fluctuated a great deal. The spinner would tie about 40 lbs of hemp around his waist, a wisp would be fastened to the wheel which the spinner boy was turning and the spinner would walk backwards paying out the hemp with his left hand while making the thread with his right. This rope walk was in Mill Road and the picture shows Mr. and Mrs. John Baker with 'Cat' Parsons in the right foreground.

37. George Green, a spinner from Staffordshire, came to Hailsham and agreed to spin yarn for Burfields whilst they continued to make the ropes. The industry prospered but in 1830 George Green decided to break away and set up his own works in Summerheath Road. The two firms remained separate until 1953 when they were re-united within the Hawkins and Tipson Group and the making of large diameter ropes in Hailsham dates from that time. In addition, the firm of Marlow Ropes was formed to specialise in the manufacture of ropes for yachting. The photograph shows a rope-walk on the Summerheath Road site.

38. The name 'trug' is believed to derive from the Old English word 'trog', meaning tub or boat. Although nowadays trug making is confined mainly to Herstmonceux and East Hoathly, at one time it was also carried out by Green Brothers. The body is made from thin slats of willow, seven or nine in number, while the rim and handle are made from ash or chestnut, copper nails being used to fasten the whole basket together. The tools used for this craft nowadays are basically the same as can be seen in this picture of a Green Brothers trugmaker sitting astride his 'horse' and nailing the first board to the frame. The pile of boards at his side will have had their ends thinned and narrowed slightly to ensure a good fit before being steamed to make them pliable.

39. During the 1914-1918 War Green Brothers were involved in a great deal of work for the Government. Amongst other things they wove camouflage screening, made sails, kite balloon screens and covers for hangar frames. Even with hangar cover sheds floor space was insufficient and two acres of meadowland were frequently covered by canvas sheets in the process of manufacture during the summer months. This picture shows the grommets being fixed to a hangar cover. Tent pegs were another product and over 200 acres of woodland were cut down to supply 100,000 poles used in making 2¼ million tent pegs between 1915 and 1918. During the War of 1939-1945 they were engaged in making dummy aircraft for deployment on decoy airfields.

40. Less than 1,500 civilians were killed by enemy action from sea or air during the 1914-1918 War but some 150,000 English people died of influenza in the winter of 1918/19 from an epidemic which started in the Near East and spread across the world. Green Brothers were still engaged on important war work for the government and could not afford to have their workforce decimated so they provided all their staff with a daily dose of quinine. The bitter taste of the medicine was partially disguised by adding cinnamon and here Mr. J. Gurr is seen administering the daily doses at what came to be known as the 'cinnamon parade'. It is reported to have been very effective which is just as well because about three-quarters of the population were affected by the epidemic.

41. In 1252 King Henry III granted a Charter *to our dear and faithful Peter of Savoy and his heirs in perpetuity to have a market in his manor of Haylesham every week on Wednesday.* It was held on the High Street from 1252 to 1638 but was then discontinued until 1786. In that year it was re-established and continued to be held on the High Street until the present site in Market Street became available. During the thirteenth century market tolls were taken and devoted to garrison expenses at Pevensey Castle. By 1834 Hailsham had become one of the greatest cattle and corn markets in Sussex and drovers accompanied their cattle from as far afield as Wales. As early as 1845 the traders in the High Street were complaining of the oak rails and hurdles which were left in position more or less permanently.

42. In 1862 the Hailsham Cattle Market Company Limited was formed to provide a new cattle and livestock market. An area of approximately three acres of land was leased from the Duke of Devonshire and in 1868 the existing office, brick walls, entrance gate and wooden cattle rails were erected at a cost of £500. When the market had been held on the High Street the buying and selling of stock had been done by private agreement and there was some opposition from the farmers to the selling by auction which was introduced on the new site because this involved the payment of commission to the auctioneers.

43. Even after the market day congestion in the High Street had disappeared due to the use of the site in Market Street, it was still a common sight to see cattle making their way along the streets in the centre of the town such as these entering Market Square from Market Street unlike today when they are all transported by vehicle to and from market. Indeed, cattle were still being brought to market 'on the hoof' as late as 1949 or 1950. The facing building on the right of the picture at one time was the Post Office but today is the Midland Bank premises. The building on the left — at the corner of Vicarage Road — was demolished in 1937.

44. The London, Brighton and South Coast Railway Company constructed a line from Polegate to Hailsham which was opened on 14th May, 1849. The opening of the line was saddened by the death of John Hield of Bexhill who was killed whilst standing on the step of a railway carriage and was struck by the level crossing gate at Mulbrooks. Originally there was a platform on the down side only, a second platform (connected by a sub-way) being provided for the up direction when the line was extended northwards to Heathfield in 1880. The Stationmaster's house, seen on the left of the picture, was completed in mid-1892 and is still standing today although the rest of the station buildings were demolished shortly after the line was closed in 1968.

45. This view of the front of the Station buildings with the locomotive shed at the left of the picture must have been taken not later than 1880 because in that year the ornamental belfry over the centre roof was removed. The coming of the railway made a vast difference to the lives of the people of Hailsham and travel to Eastbourne became more commonplace. At the turn of the century a 3rd Class return to Eastbourne cost 9d. (less than 4p.) and it was possible to leave Victoria by the 5.45 train and arrive in Hailsham by 7.45 at a cost of 6s.3d. (just over 31p.). Goods were now coming by train including building materials such as the Welsh slate used for roofing many of the buildings constructed at that time. In addition there were special arrangements for cattle traffic on market days and a coal yard was established on what is now a housing estate.

46. When the Railway was extended northwards to Heathfield it cut across the footpath used by residents walking to and from the town and by children going to and from the school in Battle Road. In 1894 at the Easter Vestry meeting — soon to be replaced by the Parish Council — Mr. James Maryan called for provision of a bridge over the railway at Eastwell Path but it was not built until 1914. Until then people had needed either to use steps provided at each side of the steep cutting or to make a comparatively lengthy detour and on one occasion five small children were seen 'sitting like swallows on the rails'.

47. London, Brighton & South Coast Railway locomotive No. 76, 'Hailsham', is seen here taking on water. It was completed at Brighton Works in June, 1877 and was stationed at Hailsham for working the Hailsham-Polegate trains, of which there were eleven each way on weekdays and six on Sundays. At some time after the line was extended northwards from Hailsham in 1880, No. 76 was transferred to Eastbourne, the end of whose nameboard can just be seen on the platform at the right-hand side of the picture. No. 76 was one of a class of fifty locomotives designed by William Stroudley, costing an average £1,875 to build and nicknamed 'Terriers' because of their small size and tenacious character. 'Hailsham' was scrapped in 1903 but several of the class can still be seen on the Kent & East Sussex Railway and the Bluebell Railway.

THE COUNCIL SCHOOLS - HAILSHAM

48. The Board School in Battle Road was opened in September, 1878 and accommodated about three hundred children. It was built at a cost of £3,000 to replace the National School which had been built in 1827 on the Common but was closed in 1878 because it was in the way of the proposed extension of the railway towards Heathfield. The Hailsham School Board had been set up under the 1870 Education Act to provide school places for all children in the area not already attending voluntary schools. The Board Schools were financed out of the rates with an annual Government inspection. The children would be examined by a visiting Inspector and the number of passes obtained would determine the amount of money made available which was supplemented by an attendance grant for each child who had attended for one hundred days during the year.

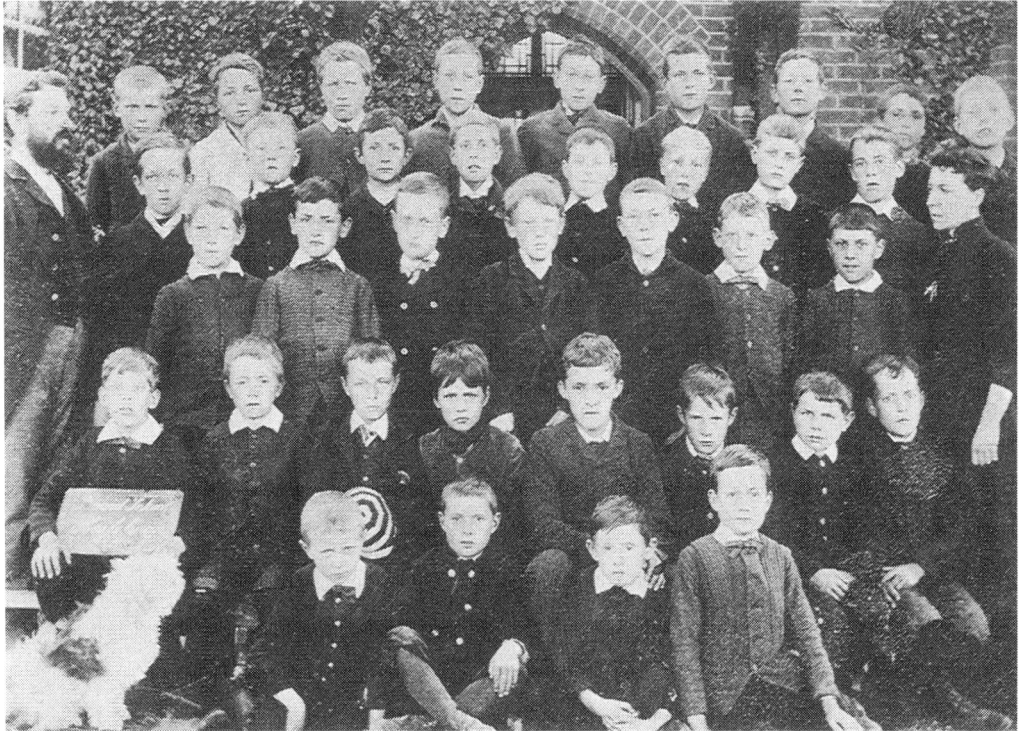

49. When the Board School opened in 1878, it operated as separate schools for boys and girls. Mr. Charles Towler was appointed from 173 applicants as Master of the boys' school and his wife was appointed as Mistress of the girls' school. Allowance was made for two hundred and forty pupils in the initial intake of the combined schools but attendance was far from perfect and the attendance rate was only 61% in 1887. Children would be absent for harvesting, hopping and blackberry gathering and also for such occasions as the Band of Hope annual outing, Temperance Fetes and the Juvenile Oddfellows sports. In addition, epidemics were frequent – such as scarlet fever, diphtheria and measles – and these led to temporary closures of the school. The photograph shows Mr. Towler with some of his pupils in the late 1880's.

50. Cricket was played on Hailsham Common until 1830, the earliest recorded match taking place on 25th August, 1788 between the Gentlemen of Hailsham and the Gentlemen of Herstmonceux for half a guinea a man, starting at 10 a.m. and playing to a finish. The Club in its present form has continuous records from 1884 and the group of players, shown here, is from about 1895. The striped blazers must have provided a colourful sight while the knotted ties used to support trousers would be frowned upon today. William Crocker, on the extreme right of the picture, looks the personification of the village blacksmith, which indeed he was.

51. Hailsham Cricket Club have always held their Cricket Week during the first full week in August but it was not until 1909 that they had a Pavilion for their use, renting the land on which it stood from the Parish Council at an annual rental of one shilling. The agreement between the Cricket Club and the Parish Council was terminated in 1955 and replaced by an arrangement whereby the Club transferred the Pavilion to the Parish Council in return for rent free use of the building so long as the Club continued 'under its existing constitution and for its present objects'. The Pavilion was erected for £300 which was raised by various subscriptions, fêtes, concerts, and jumble sales.

52. It is recorded in the Parish Registers that in 1625 Edward Willforde *fell down dead as he was playing a match of football on the Sabbath Day,* so the game has a long history in Hailsham. The present club was formed in 1885, being founder members of the East Sussex League in the 1890's and winners of the Sussex Junior Cup in 1895/96. In the early days the players changed at the Terminus Hotel and then walked to the Recreation Ground to play, travelling to away games by bicycle or pony and cart. At the time of the photograph club colours were hooped black and white shirts, thus earning the team the nickname of 'The Magpies'.

53. This Edwardian photograph shows a group of tennis players on the Recreation Ground, Western Road. The building in the background is Wellington House — nowadays known as Southview — which was presented to the Parish by the Green family as a library and reading-room in memory of Ewart Green, who was killed in action during the 1914-1918 War. The tennis courts were in the south-eastern corner of the Recreation Ground and, because they were not surrounded by wire netting, small boys could earn a few pennies by retrieving balls for the players. Previously, tennis had been played on a plot of land in Western Road opposite to the property known as Boynton.

54. As a result of a meeting in 1901 the Hailsham Band was formed and townspeople contributed to purchase instruments and uniforms. Sixteen brass instruments and two drums were obtained for £73.13s.3d. and seventeen uniforms for 36/- each. The first conductor was aptly named Mr. Trill. In 1906 the band was disbanded due to quarrelling about the severity of fines such as 'smoking in the practice room (fine 1d.)' and 'using profane language (fine 3d.)'. After six months the band restarted and was in great demand for local events and competed successfully in Band Contests. One young man, George Colwell, after playing with the band went on to obtain his A.R.C.M. and become a bandmaster in the Royal Marines. In 1940 it was evident that the band could not continue with depleted numbers due to war conditions so it was amalgamated with other bandsmen from Heathfield, Warbleton and Chiddingly and continued to function as the British Legion and Home Guard Band.

55. The picture shows the Hailsham Harriers at the New Inn, Hadlow Down, about 1895. The pack had origins dating back to 1823 and their earliest Master, Richard King Sampson, lived at Hope Villa, Western Road — later to be rebuilt as Summerfields House. Later Masters included Algernon Pitcher and Holland Southerden, both local yeomen. In the early days of the present century the blue mottle hounds enjoyed a national reputation. Their kennels at the time were on land now part of the school playing fields in Battle Road. They were disbanded in the 1914-1918 War. Old Bridger, their huntsman, is reputed to have boasted that at the age of seventy he had every tooth in his head still whole. Their country is now hunted by the Pevensey Marsh Beagles.

56. Around the turn of the century the scissors grinder and his barrow was a familiar sight in any town or village. Old Mayes was a well-known character in Hailsham and the surrounding area. Unfortunately, he had a habit of getting drunk and sometimes when in this condition his barrow would be hidden by the local lads. On one occasion it had been placed in the middle of the Vicarage lawn and, while Old Mayes was looking for his barrow in the bushes at St. Wilfrid's, he was accosted by the Vicar, the Reverend F. Clyde Harvey. 'Mayes', said the Vicar, 'if you want your barrow, it is on the Vicarage lawn and there are also six pairs of scissors which want grinding.' The photograph shows Old Mayes with his barrow outside St. Wilfrid's.

57. This photograph of four oxen drawing a Sussex farm wagon past Sturton Place and the Terminus Hotel reminds us of the important part played by these animals in local agriculture from Roman times and they were still being used during the 1914-1918 War. They were slower than the horse but needed fewer rests so were able to plough the same acreage and their basic diet of oat straw made them economical to keep. They were broken into work at two years of age, worked for six or seven years and then were fattened for slaughter. The same spans – or pairs – were always harnessed together. The distance measurement of a furlong – derived from 'furrow long' – was that which the ox-team could plough before it rested at the headland. The man leading the animals is carrying a long 'goad' to encourage them to keep moving.

58. With its strong Puritan tradition East Sussex has always been a stronghold of November 5th celebrations complete with bonfires, fireworks and fancy dress. Hailsham was no exception and the Committee of 1897 seem determined to set a good example. There would be two processions by the Bonfire Boys winding up with a bonfire on the Recreation Ground. They were not popular with all sections of the population and one year the date of a meeting of the Mutual Improvement Guild was altered as it was felt that the proceedings on Guy Fawke's Day would hardly encourage ladies to venture out. In 1901 the Committee of the Hailsham Brass Band declined an invitation by the Bonfire Society to take part in the proceedings because to do so might seriously affect the future support to the funds of the Band.

59. There was great activity in the town with preparations for the coronation of King Edward VII and Queen Alexandra. Most of the shop fronts, as this one at 49, High Street, were elaborately decorated and illuminated and many activities were planned for the actual day. The church bells would ring from 6 a.m. until 8 a.m. and the Hailsham Band would play on Market Square. After the service in the Parish Church there would be a procession of decorated conveyances, Friendly Societies, the Fire Brigade, the Band and all school children. The old folks were to have a dinner and after the sports events the children would have tea. During the evening would be a bonfire and pyrotechnic display. Unfortunately due to the illness of the King the Coronation was postponed from 26th June until 9th August so the dinner and tea took place as planned but the other events were at the later date.

60. On the 27th June, 1894, Austin's gun shop on the High Street was burnt to the ground. Four years later the land was acquired by the Parish Council for about £190 and the public were asked to contribute towards the cost. The idea for gates was also mooted but interest in the scheme declined. The death of Queen Victoria on 22nd January 1901 brought renewed interest to the scheme and it was decided to erect the gates in her memory. On the 9th December that year there was an opening ceremony and a dedication service. The pillars were constructed of Portland stone to match the church tower. This picture shows the gates decorated for the coronation of King Edward VII and Queen Alexandra in 1902.

61. The end of the Boer War in 1902 was greeted with great rejoicing. As soon as the news was confirmed in Hailsham on Sunday, June 1st the Church bells rang a joyful peal and people gathered in the Market Square. The following morning, the town began to be decked out with flags and preparations were made for a gala day. A hastily formed Committee improvised sports and cricket on the Recreation Ground in the afternoon and there was a torchlight procession in the evening with a small display of fireworks. At that time Charles Underwood Jenner lived at 11, High Street – it was then known as The Acacias and the modern shopfront was added later – and we can see that he had entered fully into the spirit of the celebrations.

62. Beating the Bounds is a custom of great antiquity dating back to the time when there were very few maps and it was necessary for representatives of a parish to walk the boundaries of their area annually to establish that there had been no encroachments. These walks were also known as Perambulations or Rogations and Rogation week is always that in which Ascension Day occurs. When this photograph was taken at Leap Cross about 1910, the parish of Hailsham (based on the ecclesiastical parish) included much of what is today in the parish of Polegate and a walk of about twenty-five miles was involved – taking about eight hours to complete – compared with the modern parish perimeter of about sixteen miles. At suitable points the boys were 'bumped' in order to instil into their memories the actual boundary. The boundary went through the middle of a farmhouse at one place and the smallest boy was passed through the pantry window.

63. When war was declared on 4th August, 1914 the 2nd Home Counties (Sussex) Brigade, Royal Field Artillery, comprising three batteries and an ammunition column, was called to war stations at Eastbourne, Hastings, Bexhill, and Hailsham. The seaside towns supplied the horses and men to draw and man the guns while Hailsham and the surrounding villages supplied most of the men, horses, wagons and carts for the ammunition column. Officers and parties of men were sent round the farms to commandeer horses and wagons — sometimes actually taking the horses as they were working in the fields — and bring them into the town where the horses were tethered in long lines in the Deer Paddock and the Vicarage Field. This picture, which shows some of the horses at the Deer Paddock, was chosen by Mr. and Mrs. C.H. Green for their Christmas card that year — a most unusual choice by present day standards.

64. A group of men of the 5th (Territorial) Battalion Royal Sussex Regiment at the Tower of London in 1914. Many of the men shown here come from the Hailsham area. The sergeant in the centre with the walking stick was Hugh Roberts who survived the war and was awarded the Distinguished Conduct Medal for bravery in action. A school teacher, he spent all his teaching life at Battle Road School. Hugh Marillier, another teacher at the same school and in the same battalion, was also awarded the D.C.M. but sadly was killed in action. Sergeant-Major Nelson Carter, once a pupil at Battle Road School, was awarded a posthumous Victoria Cross. The Royal Sussex Regiment suffered terrible casualties at the Battle of Aubers Ridge in 1915 and Aubers Ridge day is still kept as an anniversary in the Regiment. They were known as The Iron Regiment.

65. Hailsham Liberal Association was formed in December 1923. The Committee appear to have spent a great deal of time organising jumble sales and fêtes to raise funds and providing outings for the Young Liberals. A highlight, in 1925, was a visit from the Rt. Hon. D. Lloyd George who is seen in this picture in Market Square, speaking in support of the Liberal Candidate (W. Harcourt Johnson) at the By-Election.

66. The inhabitants of Hailsham, recognising their indebtedness to the Princess Alice Memorial Hospital in Eastbourne, decided to show their gratitude in a practical manner. A meeting was held on the 4th August, 1898 and the Hailsham Hospital Committee was formed to collect funds for the hospital which was a Free Institution and depended entirely on voluntary contributions. On a Wednesday during August six tables would be placed at strategic places in the town and here the good ladies of the committee would collect money from passers-by. The following Saturday there would be a house-to-house collection and on the Sunday a procession composed of church and civic dignitaries, all the Friendly Societies and the Fire Brigade would march to the Recreation Ground for an open-air service. The townspeople gave generously and the first year the Committee sent over £54 to the Princess Alice Hospital.

ILSHAM UNION. 28.

67. Until 1834 each Parish had its own Poor House, many dating back to Elizabethan times, but under the Poor Law Amendment Act of that year Unions of Parishes were set up. The Hailsham Union comprised the parishes of Arlington, Chiddingly, Hailsham, Heathfield, Hellingly, Herstmonceux, Hooe, Laughton, Ninfield, Warbleton and Wartling with Chalvington and Ripe being added in 1898. The Central House, seen here, was on the Hellingly side of Hawks Road while the Guardians met in the Board Room on the Hailsham side of the road. There was always a problem with drinking water and a new 100 feet deep well costing £117 was dug in 1881; the pump wheel has been preserved and can still be seen outside the Museum in Western Road. The workhouse closed in 1932 and was demolished to be replaced by bungalows and houses.

Wishing you a happy Christmas.

Hellingly Asylum

68. Towards the end of 1897 an area of four hundred acres at Park Farm, Hellingly was offered to Sussex County Council for £16,000 by the Earl of Chichester as the site for an Asylum, the estimated cost of which was £207,000. The Hospital, known to old Hellingly residents as 'The Top', was opened in 1903 as the East Sussex County Mental Hospital and remained as such until the National Health Service was introduced in 1948. It is now the Psychiatric Hospital for a large area of East Sussex and Kent and provides accommodation for some 1,400 patients with a further 60 at Amberstone Hospital. The tall brick chimney is a familiar landmark.

69. Horselunges Manor is a moated timber-framed house built by a member of the Devenish family at the end of the fifteenth century and restored in 1925. The name Horselunges is a corruption of Herstlyngyver which in turn was a combination of the family names of Philip de Herst and Agnes Lyngyver. The house was sold in 1568 to the Pelham family who retained it until the early part of the present century. What remains today is only part of one side of a larger, perhaps quadrangular, house of which the original hall has disappeared. The photograph shows the house as it was at the turn of the century without the large gabled windows of the present day.

70. The interior of Horselunges Manor has much fine timber, especially the very large tie beams. The photograph, which was taken about 1930, shows only a part of the Great Chamber in which it is reputed to have been possible to turn a horse and wagon. Behind the Manor is a field known as Pick Hay which was the scene of a tragic incident in 1541. Lord Dacre of Herstmonceux Castle went poaching deer with some of his friends on land owned by Nicholas Pelham. They were surprised by Pelham gamekeepers, one of whom was fatally wounded in the subsequent affray. Lord Dacre was tried and found guilty and was executed at Tyburn. It is said that this was the first time in English history that a man of noble birth was executed for killing a commoner.

71. There is a record in the Hellingly Parish Church register of a man drowning at Horsebridge Mill in 1634. A scheme was put forward in 1792 to construct a canal from the River Ouse near Beddingham to Horsebridge Mill to open up this area of Sussex for better trading but the project was abandoned. The mill was seriously damaged by fire in 1908 despite the combined efforts of the fire brigades of Hailsham and Eastbourne, the latter's horse-drawn pump arriving with steam up and ready to pump only twenty-five minutes after receiving the call. The mill was rebuilt and remained very busy, grinding not only English corn but also Rumanian and Canadian. It passed into the ownership of Ranks Ltd. but, although still very busy, was closed by them in 1969.

72. This photograph of about 1880 shows Star Brewery Cottages which still stand today although the shop has been converted to a dwelling and a new shop has been built nearby. The shop was an off-licence and grocery business. Not only was beer sold in bottles but customers would take their jugs to be filled from the casks, the cost up to the 1914 War varying between 2d. and 4d. per pint depending on strength. During the building of Hellingly Hospital from 1898 to 1903 there was a large influx of workmen, many of whom lived rough in barns and cattle sheds, coming to the shop for their beer and provisions. They would take their beer across the road and drink it sitting on tree trunks and stacks of sawn timber in Pitcher's timber yard which came to be known as the 'open air bar'. Men would play marbles in front of the shop on Good Fridays until the hour when Christ was reputed to have been nailed to the cross.

73. This photograph was taken about 1875 at Lower Horsebridge at the junction of two Turnpike roads, one known as the Horsebridge and Horeham Trust and the other as the Broyle Gate and Battle Trust. These trusts were established by an Act passed in 1754 and they ceased to operate in 1872, from which date the cost of maintaining the roads had to be met from the rates. The road at this junction was controlled by two gates joined by a central post. The photograph shows what is thought to be a part of the side fence and post after the actual gates had been removed. All signs of the gates have long since gone but the Toll House remains and is used as a shop selling antiques. The postal address of Hellingly at this period was Hellingly, Hawkhurst and mail would be received daily by horse mail from the Kentish town for sorting and delivery over the large surrounding area.

74. The present front of the King's Head conceals a much older rear and at one time it was a coaching inn with stables for a large number of horses, being at the junction of two turnpike roads. The inn was the meeting place of the Manor Courts and the Turnpike Trustees and also auction sales of local farms and properties were held there. Nearby a cattle fair was held each year on May 9th and September 29th. The Hon. John Byng (later Lord Torrington) stayed overnight in 1788 and noted that supper was eaten in a room 36 feet by 21 feet. The photograph is about 1910 and shows the travelling fishmonger who made his way from the coast to nearby inland villages selling his fresh fish.

The Dicker, Sussex 266.

75. It is not known when pottery making first started in the area known as The Dicker but there is a record of the setting up of a second pottery in 1774. Before that date there may have been a connection with Michelham Priory where pottery was known to have been made in mediaeval times. The works which became known as the Dicker Pottery are believed to have been acquired by the Clark family in about 1845. The Boship Pottery closed down at the turn of the century and the owner joined the Dicker Pottery. Uriah Clark, who died in 1903, did not confine himself to pottery and at various times was described also as a grocer and draper and coal and coke merchant. The business became the private limited company of Uriah Clark and Nephew in 1912 and remained so until 1941 when the buildings and land were requisitioned by the Army. The pottery was re-opened by a new owner after the War but was finally closed in the 1950's.

SUSSEX POTTERY: FLOWER POT MAKING.

76. Apart from the vases, crockery and other items usually associated with a pottery, the Dicker Pottery also produced goods such as bricks, tiles, pipes, chimney pots and flower pots. In 1927 a report stated that there was enough clay on the site to last a small brickmaking firm for hundred years but the owners chose to put all their efforts into the existing pottery. The most popular ware produced there was reminiscent of sixteenth century Cistercian and was coated with a black lustre iron glaze but it did not possess the robustness of the pots made for everyday use. The Pottery, which had two kilns, provided employment for about twenty persons.